Dr Paulus

Magicon

Wonderful Prophecies concerning popery and its impending overthrow and fall

Dr Paulus

Magicon
Wonderful Prophecies concerning popery and its impending overthrow and fall

ISBN/EAN: 9783337064259

Printed in Europe, USA, Canada, Australia, Japan

Cover: Foto ©ninafisch / pixelio.de

More available books at **www.hansebooks.com**

Magicon:

WONDERFUL PROPHECIES CONCERNING

POPERY

and its impending Overthrow and Fall,

TOGETHER WITH

Predictions relative to America,

THE

'End of the World

AND THE

Formation of the New Earth;

ALSO, CONCERNING THE TRUE BEGINNING AND FUTURE OF

The New Church, called the New Jerusalem.

With Twenty-four Magic Figures.

By Dr. PAULUS.

New York, 1869.

Entered according to Act of Congress, in the year 1868,

By Dr. PAULUS,

In the Clerk's Office, of the District Court of the United States for the Southern District of New York.

John J. Reed, Book and Job Printer, 43 Centre St., N. Y.

Introduction.

~~~~~~~~

————————" As the sun,
Ere it is risen, sometimes paints its image
In the atmosphere, so often do the spirits
Of great events stride on before the events,
And in to-day already walks to-morrow."
SCHILLER (Wallenstein.)

THERE IS A GOD!—All nature proclaims His existence; it is echoed forth with ten thousand, thousand voices, from the countless works of His hand, throughout this stupendous universe! The whole history of man bears witness to the truth that there is a God; we see it inscribed on every page, in sublime and eternal characters. Never, indeed, has mankind entirely lost this sacred creed, although it has, at times, been obscured, by passing from one nation, tribe, or generation, to another.

With the belief in the existence of a Supreme Being, are all the highest aspirations of the human soul most intimately interwoven. Every achievement of man, however lofty and sublime, will— if not resting on the everlasting pillars of this glorious creed—appear, with all its grandeur, but little better than the empty and trifling pastimes of a child! In vain do we try to search out His grandeur, by scrutinizing with our microscopes the infinitely small; nor shall we, thinking to have found in the laws of motion a clue to His never-ceasing creative power, discover His throne amid the interminable space. This puerile searching in the material world serves only to lead us astray from our true path—from the path of light and *spiritual* understanding. Of what avail are the diplomacy and state-craft of the so-called civilized nations, whose giant structures of polity, reared with so much subtlety, and with so many hecatombs of victims, we behold crumbling to pieces on every side! And that vast accumulation of philosophical works, which we are wont to admire as master-pieces of the human intellect, one of which refutes another—what are they, but a proof that all and every thing conceived without the Spirit of God, must sooner or later come to naught!

This has been the mode in which all reasoning minds have looked at history, ever since its beginning. Still we see eminent men who, eagerly grasping after the unknown, lose their foothold at the very moment they thought themselves nearest the victory.

Where shall we look for the reason why these great minds still persevere in searching in the dark, without ever discovering the truth, the fountain of all wisdom? Oh! ye wise men, North, South, East, and West, why do you not acknowledge that the real cause of the vanity and fruitlessness of your researches lies in your turning away from Him who is the Lord of hosts, the Creator of the universe, the Ruler of the destinies of man? But men have ears, and hear not; they have eyes, and see not. They see not the hand, now stretching forth from among the clouds to shower blessings on His true and loving children, and now, in a thousand varying ways, sending punishment upon His disobedient creatures, who deny their God, and refuse to love their fellow-men. They hear not the voice of the Father revealing itself in the fruit-nourishing shower, in the growing seed, in the thirst-quenching draught. They cannot see that by the abundance of blessings which He bestows upon us, He wishes to kindle in our souls the desire for brotherly love. They hear not His voice of thunder; they hear it not in the howling storm, in the surging of the destroying waves, in the agonies of innumerable victims, dying unsoothed by human aid or sympathy, in times of direful pestilence. They hear it not as it calls them to turn again to Him, again to seek the ways of truth, to become men, loving brethren, and His faithful and submissive children.

There are voices which we may even now hear, through which he speaks to us, revealing His holy will—even the voices of the Prophets.

Prophecies and Revelations.

The belief in supernatural revelations is as old as the belief in God; we find it not only among Christians, but also among the heathen, although they may adore their God under the form of a Fetish. Cicero, who has written a long treatise on revelation, says : " There is a belief among all nations, handed down from the heroic times, that there exists among men the gift of prophesying, or rather a presentment, a knowledge of things to come." A glorious gift, indeed, which in frail mortals approaches the Divine Power.

I find no people, be it ever so humane and so highly civilized, or ever so brutish and degraded, which does not believe in a foreshadowing of future events, capable of being discerned and interpreted by some of their fellow men. Is it not wrong in us to set aside that which has been handed down from, and hallowed through time immemorial ?

Among the ancients, we find no nation more addicted to this belief, and more firm in their conviction in regard to supernatural revelation, than the Greeks. They said that the Gods, knowing the Future and the Past, reveal them to men, either freely out of love, or being prevailed upon by prayers, and that they sometimes give them signs for their guidance.

Plato, in his Phædrus and Phædon, holds this opinion to be true : that the soul of man participates in its Divine attributes, and that it therefore is not subject to the same laws of nature as the body ; but that, since the soul has sinned in a premundane life, it has been degraded to a bodily nature, so that thereby also its original faculty of spiritual and prophetic vision has been dimmed. *Not entirely, however, have men lost their power of supernatural vision, because, from its very nature, that power is indestructible.*

Says *Plutarch*, in a very striking passage: "Like the sun, which does not merely become brilliant after emerging from the clouds, but is thus at all times, and only on account of the vapors surrounding it ever appears dark to us: so also the soul does not only, on emerging from the body as from a cloud, regain its power of looking into the future, but it possesses that power even now; obscured, however, or dimmed, as it were, by its present mixture and union with the mortal frame." Hence this inalienable gift of the soul, lying dormant as it does during the common course of life, may under certain favorable circumstances become free and active. And in reality, there are some conditions of the human frame which allow of a more or less free action of the soul: *Such conditions are sleep, dreams, and certain diseases.*

Xenophon says: "During sleep, the souls of men appear freest and most God-like, and cast a glance into the future." *Josephus:* "During sleep, the souls of men, nowise distracted by the body, enjoy sweetest repose, are in close contact and communion with God, to whom they are akin, go everywhere and see future events." Examples to serve as proof of the above, abound in the literature of Magnetism. It is not, however, the object or intention of this book to produce such evidence, since already a great many voluminous works have been written, containing the record of actual experiences to that effect, which will afford ample information to those who may desire to learn more regarding these subjects.

Equally well known is the fact that under the influence of certain *diseases*, the faculty of seeing visions, or the power of clairvoyance, is developed. *Inflammatory* diseases, particularly those of the brain, occasion as it were a delirium of a prophetic nature. Most of the nervous affections, especially hysterics, chorea, and epilepsy, furnish numerous instances of this sort. *Betulus* mentions an epileptic boy who, after attacks of this nature, was accustomed to be thrown into a state, during the continuance of which he told of extraordinary things, even of the condition of the departed. When awakened from such an attack, he asserted positively that he had conversed with angels; that he had walked in the most enchanting gardens, enjoying indescribable felicity. These, indeed, are statements such as magnetizers have had occasion frequently to hear from those put into magnetic sleep.

Nor are prophetic gifts of rare occurrence among *lunatics*. That maniacs have often been worshiped as saints, may be accounted for by this fact. We frequently hear of illiterate men in lunatic asylums bursting forth into songs, the language of which is in the highest degree elevated and refined. Thus *Tasso* wrote his delightful verses during his most violent attacks: so did *Lucretius*. *Babeuf* is said to have composed his most enchanting poems during paroxysms of intense fever. *Claws*, the celebrated fool, once entered suddenly into the Hall where the secret

Council of Weimar was holding its session, and exclaimed: "There you are deliberating about great things, but none of you thinks of putting down the conflagration at Coburg." And truly, the first news confirmed the reality of what he had thus announced.

In *consumptive* patients likewise, the prophetic gift has been found. Thus, *Keizer* tells us of a man dying of this disease, who before the outbreak of the French Revolution predicted its whole course. It seems to be an old experience that dying men generally prophesy.

The oldest authors, such as *Hippocrates, Galen, Avicenna, Aretœus, Cicero, Plutarch*, make mention of numerous instances of this fact. *Plutarch* very truly remarks, in consequence of an observaation of this nature, that "the soul does not acquire a new faculty after death, which it had not already possessed before. Only dimmed in the body, it merely reassumes its power when the vital qualities diminish, and the weary limbs oppress it no longer."

But strongest of all do we see the gift of prophesy among *magnetic patients*, or so called *somnambulists*. They constitute, as it were, the connecting link between those who prophesy whilst sound in body, and those who only acquire this gift when in a diseased condition. We are inclined to number among the latter those gifted with what is called the "*second sight*"; in Gælic, *Taishitraugh* (*Taish*, spectre, and *Taishatrin*, seen.) For those who are less familiar with the nature and phenomena of the second sight, we will give the following

short description. The very moment that the seer
falls into this extraordinary condition—which may
happen at any time, day as well as night—he suddenly becomes rigid, stiff; his eyes are closed;
often, however, they remain open, and in this case
he looks steadily in one direction, with a fixed,
staring glance. Hearing and seeing are lost in
regard to all that takes place around him. The
mind, however, acquires an astounding power of
penetration, whereby it overcomes every obstacle
from the material world, and pierces in full freedom alike into the past, present, and future, which
all pass with an unusual vividness in rapid succession before his view. The death or arrival of persons often hundreds of miles distant, events taking
place in remote localities, such as battles, naval
engagements, conflagrations, are then announced
by the seer, and described with marvellous accu-
racy. In such moments, his language is often
poetical, symbolic, always powerful and impres-
sive, well chosen, as to style and diction, majestic
and sublime. By contact with foot or hand, these
visions may be transferred from one person to another. Even persons distant from one another,
may have the same sight at the same moment.
Strange it is that such a seer, on going to foreign
countries, loses this gift, which on his return seems
to be restored to him.

From *dreams* and *somnambulism* the *second sight*
differs in this, that the seer preserves a full knowledge of what he has seen in his mind, and that
this *second sight* may be said to take place while
the person is waking. From the common *ghost*

seeing it is also to be distinguished ; for in the former state the seer is in full possession of his senses, while in the latter an abnormal condition occurs, such as convulsion, rigidity, and stupor. On the Scottish Islands, second sight appears to have become less frequent during the last one hundred years; we meet with it more frequently, however, in Denmark. These seers may easily be recognized among other people by their peculiar and very piercing glance.

The perfection of clairvoyance, or faculty of seeing visions is, however, unquestionably the *prophetic trance. Ennemoser* says: " We should not confound this entranced state of the true, God-inspired seer, with the abnormal and morbid visions of the penitent Hindoo juggler, or with the crazy convulsions of religious fanatics." Here the origin, cause, appearance, and final end are different. In all anomalous conditions of the body, the mental vision is under cosmic influences, like the lightning piercing a cloud ; a storm, which has come we know not whence, blows the fire of the entranced into a blaze, and it dies away again just as suddenly. It has no definite duration, no real significance, no aim.

The ecstasy of the true prophets, on the contrary, belongs to and gives evidence of a higher order of things, reaching into the material world of man, producing in him a quiet though deep emotion, and a mild, refreshing self-illumination. The soul, awakened by the breath of the Almighty, can no longer be hindered by natural barriers from seeing and acting. No longer are its visions clouded by dream-like appearances, as is the case in the seeing of ghosts; no longer do false apparitions arise before the mind freed from pain, restlessness and fear. The body ceases to be a burden, encumbered by sickly convulsions or feverish paroxysms, and becomes, even in its weakness, an instrument and a mighty means *for work and action*, bestowing blessings on all who live in the time of the prophet, as well as on after ages.

In the *magic ecstasy* of the Brahminic jugglers, and in the fanaticism of hermits and flagellants in the Thebaide, we find the gift of seeing visions, or clairvoyance, and the pretended communication with their God, effected by particular means or clandestine practices. To the true Prophet, however, the heavenly call comes unsought from above. With the former vanity, the desire of increasing their own importance, and of appearing greater in their own eyes, seems to be the principal motive. They withdraw into dark places and deserts; they renounce the world and all society of their fellow-creatures, as well as all culture of the mind. The Prophet, however, is meek and humble, enjoys life and the good and open light of day, while the main-spring of his activity is manifested in *dealing openly, and consists in a desire to do the work.* The prophet preaches the Word of God for the purpose of awakening a belief in His supreme power, and for the sake of strengthening such a faith. He reduces good and bad actions to their true value, by showing forth their nature and consequences. He openly preaches the love of God and the love of our neighbor. In meekness a child, in active energy a youth, in wisdom a mature man—such is the true prophet. To those whom we call entranced, the world often is an irksome burden ; to the prophet it is a school. In it he learns his duties, and becomes a useful member of the human brotherhood. With the former, the means of becoming entranced, are despising and renouncing the world, and the practice of bodily castigation. With the latter, the world forms the arena for his action. He uses life rightly, and as for means by which to become entranced, the true prophet needs none. He teaches the Word of God to his fellow creatures, without killing his body. He imparts instruction to his fellow-men as readily as he lives among them.

In our account of supernatural extasies we should not forget to mention the *stigmatizing of the entranced*. This is one of the strangest phenomena in the domain of mysticism. We frequently find it among the Catholic population of Austria, Bavaria and Tyrol. Religious fanatics, on certain days in the year, actually sweat blood in the form of Christ's wounds ; they pretend to hold conversation with the saints, also with Mary, the Mother of God, and even with God himself. These being undeniable facts, we can certainly not call such strange occurrences in question, and in their presence many a learned skeptic has lost his power of reasoning, as was the case with Maria von More in Kaldern, Tyrol. All these supernatural *phenomena*, with all their wonders, can be readily discerned to be of a like nature with what in olden times they used to call " being possessed by the Devil." The influence of wicked spirits, among others those of priests, is plainly manifest in these dazzling and shifting appearances of truth and falsehood, in those abrupt pictures made up of inharmonious colors, in convulsions and contortions of the body and soul. We may therefore take it for granted that the *visions* seen by such fanatics are always unreliable, and seldom is there coherency or meaning to be found in them.

It is the same *with the phenomena of so-called*

𝔖𝔭𝔦𝔯𝔦𝔱𝔲𝔞𝔩𝔦𝔰𝔪,

with all its manifestations, and with what are styled its " *Mediums*." Were those men who make it their business to experiment in such things, to know with how *dangerous* a supernatural power they are dealing in these attempts, they certainly would refrain from following this system of Satanic falsehood,—nay, they would keep their unnatural curiosity within bounds. It would be a vain and useless task, without any definite result, to investigate all the various phases of modern Spiritualism, and to prove their real or pretended value. For its wonders are facts incontrovertible and well ascertained by every observer sound in mind and unbiased in judgment. The real problem is to find the true meaning, aim and purpose of these mysterious phenomena.

Their explanation consists essentially in the fact of a connection of a portion of the spiritual world with a corresponding portion of mankind on earth, or rather of an intercourse between men still living, and others who have either recently, or at some distant period in the past, departed this life. This intercourse is effected by means of certain persons who are, to a greater or less extent, possessed by a distinct class of spirits. These persons are called " *Mediums.*"

Such spirits, however, are evil spirits of various kinds, and be.ong to the lower or very lowest sphere of the spiritual world. For, only such does the Lord allow in our days, or rather since the Last Judgment, which took place in 1757,— to hold intercourse with men on earth, and this intercourse is possible only with those who are like those spirits, wickedly inclined or addicted to evil. No good can result from the mutual attraction between such allies ; on the contrary, nothing but evil can come from evil. Nor can any truth be gained from such intercourse, but merely error and falsehood. *The Lord* does not in general permit any *good* spirit to communicate with man. Whenever that takes place (and it is a rare occurrence), it happens with His special permission, for a particular purpose and quite in another manner, of which we will speak in its proper time. From these fundamental causes, we can easily infer the effects and consequences of Spiritualism ; from evil nothing can come but evil, from falsehood nothing but falsehood. Hence we can, in a few words, sum up the aim and end of Spiritualism, viz., *the increase of all sorts of evil and wickedness, as well as of spiritual errors and*

*falsities, and their introduction among all classes
of men: and also the turning away and falling
off from the true and only God, the Ruler of
Heaven and Earth.*

The most wicked among those spirits who try
to gain an influence by means of their power over
" Mediums," are those of the departed wicked
priests. For they are unclean spirits of the most
abominable sort, full of treachery, cunning, greediness, avarice, revenge and cruelty; but they are,
at the same time, endowed with the power of
bland and insinuating speech, and perfectly possess the art of persuading and seducing; in fact,
they are now worse and far more dangerous than
they formerly were, at the time of their existence
on earth.

All this kind of spirits, without exception, try
through their particular " Mediums" to influence
first single individuals, then families, whole communities, and finally to infest entire countries,
nations and society at large. Curiosity, vanity,
pride and all sorts of selfishness serve as means
to allure their victims. They flatter the weak
through honeyed words, pleasing answers and
astounding news in the form of revelations, which,
as well as their manifold mysterious communica-
tions, have no foundation whatsoever in reality.

Still, they succeed in deceiving the people, and
like so many *trichinæ*, they know how to get a hold
of the minds of their victims, whereby they work
destruction. Do they at last succeed in gaining
the confidence of their victims,—these will find it
almost impossible to withdraw from that Satanic

influence, and to extricate themselves from the hundredfold snares which had been so cunningly devised and prepared for them.

In this whirlpool of spiritual poison, what else can we expect to find but calumny, false accusations, false arguments, the grossest lies and the most malignant machinations, in order to undermine, in the garb of apparent truth, every principle of virtue and honor among men?

How can we wonder then, if we see that often among the most intimate friends, brothers and sisters, husbands and wives, parents and children, doubts and surmises arise in regard to one another! Mistrust, antipathy, conceit, vainty, pride, domestic strife, unjust judgments, hatred, envy, persecution and even revenge and murder—such are the results.

Take heed, therefore, ye souls, of the enticements of Spiritualism, lest it succeed in gaining the ascendency over you and destroying your peace! Take heed lest ye fall from the truth!— in particular, ye souls of frail and delicate women, so easily influenced and led astray from the heavenly good which flows from Him, the Lord, and His holy Angels!

We will now, after this digression, return to the Prophecies.

With the *Prophet*, visions are nothing but the Divine light falling, as it were, upon the mirror of a pure soul which, retaining all its individuality, remains in constant communion with God and keeps up its intercourse with the world. The prophet, therefore, does not seek his blessedness in being entranced; but he finds it in the delight of his calling, in the consciousness of doing his duty by preaching the Word of God; thus, not in secluding himself from the world and disdaining his fellow-creatures, but in active life among them. We may, therefore, say that a true prophet does not lose himself in his lofty contemplations, but holds unceasing communication with God and men, by his teachings and by a useful life. *A true prophet* does apparently not differ from other men, he does not proclaim any strange and startling mysteries or disclose any wonderful secrets—but he announces the will of Him who was from the beginning and is to the end. The prophet only endeavors to instruct his neighbor in the Word of God, and therefore we find him to be such a stalwart warrior against all lies and every sort of wickedness.

We never see him engaged in worldly pursuits, nor greedy after riches, honors, or the gratification of the senses. It is the future blessedness which, under God's inspiration, he preaches to all. He is the bright beacon-light shining forth far and wide; he is the model for all—a mediator, as it were, between God and the world. Endowed with heavenly power, he is enabled to accomplish supernatural things in himself as well as in others. His are consolation, peace and serenity of mind, when exposed to trial and suffering. He warns us against impending dangers; *he heals fatal or loathsome diseases;* he succors the needy and the oppressed, which acts are but the manifestation of God within him. His aim is to make man better, to make him wiser and happier, and to promote the extension of the kingdom of the Lord. In the disdain of his own temporal welfare, we must look for the reason of his success in the belief in an all-powerful God. *Thus, he fulfils the first of the commandments, which is love to our fellow-creatures and comprises all other human virtues.*

Any one who is conversant with the spirit of the Old Testament, cannot help seeing the miraculous guidance of the chosen people, how they were repeatedly rescued through their prophets, from the danger of falling into idolatry. Also in the New Covenant, we can discern something analagous; namely, in the development and extension of Christianity, and its whole history down to our own day. For, notwithstanding the godly precepts given us by Christist, and notwithstanding the heavenly command of love which he brought so plainly to our minds and hearts, and notwithstanding even his own glorious example—the darkest errors could not be prevented from creeping into the Temple of Christianity. Deeper indeed than the heathen and the so much despised Jews, have *Christians* sunk. Traders in souls have again invaded the new-built Temple of the Lord, and have therein established their markets. There has come to be a greater and greater dearth of truth, justice, religion and love in the world, and the purest of all doctrines has given place to the basest kind of selfishness.

But the Lord has not forsaken His children; He still wishes to raise them from their deep degradation, if they will only yield themselves up to His divine guidance. But man, absorbed in the eager pursuit of material welfare, appears incapable of being awakened, except by misfortunes, sorrows and sufferings. Thus only can he be brought to look into himself; thus only does he become convinced of his faults and sensible of his own spiritual misery. He must repent; for without repentance, there is no road to goodness nor to a pure and holy life. To every one after the measure of the capacity of his soul does God send sufferings and distress, as a means to raise him from his fallen condition. Man, consisting as he does of soul and body, his suffering must necessarily be of a two-fold nature, so as to make him rise again from that degradation into which he had been dragged by the folly of his own moral weakness. For those who are yet worth saving, the sufferings are both of body and soul.

The bodily sufferings comprise all ailments of the body: pain, sickness, and the king of terrors—death! The more we indulge in the delights of our senses and the gratification of the external man, the more will our body chastise its tenant, the soul; and the more shall we feel oppressed in our mental activity.

Matter, indeed, reaps heavy vengeance for having been thus allied with its master, the soul. Weakness, diseases, malformations, and all sorts of bodily ailments, are the natural consequences *which the Lord allows, but which we bring on ourselves by our own fault,* often thereby preparing for ourselves indescribable agonies of pain.

The sufferings of the soul are disturbances,

weaknesses, diseases of the understanding, affections of the mind. The tortures from ungratified passions, such as avarice, pride, inordinate craving after honors, etc., belong to this class. So do losses, humiliations, shame, and many others. The greatest sufferings of which the soul is capable, have for their result either the meek and humble acknowledgment of having misunderstood our system of life—or the denial of God, the refusal of his aid, and a haughty over-rating of our own mental strength, ending in gross Materialism, despair and incurable madness. To the capacity of each individual are these several kinds of suffering adapted, so that also families, communities, nations, and all mankind, have to suffer in proportion.

History bears witness to the melancholy disappearance of entire nations; and as a father who educates his child, disciplines it for its transgressions, so also does the Heavenly Ruler educate His creatures, and mete out their punishments. History, viewed in this light, has been nothing but a record of the education and development of mankind, under the guidance of their Maker. The father, before inflicting punishment on his child, warns it repeatedly; he then even begins with a light punishment; and if that proves unavailing, he resorts to a heavier correction. Thus also does the Lord admonish His chosen people through His prophets and inspired seers; but if they remain deaf to these admonitions, then He first sends some smaller calamities and sufferings, before consuming His hardened and rebellious creatures in His wrath. Thus it was in the times of the Old Covenant, with the Israelites; thus it was also in the New Dispensation, when the Jews crucified their Saviour; and thus it has continued to be ever since through the whole history of mankind, down to our own day. The prophets of old, the Apostles, and many God-inspired seers who have appeared from time to time, are living witnesses to it. Nevertheless, we must not believe that all prophets are true ones; neither are all prophecies true. Jesus himself says: "Beware of *false* prophets!" Many prophecies, moreover, have been wrongly interpreted. Such are especially the vain and fanciful attempts which have been made to explain the Revelation of St. John. All times which are full of great and important events, have their prophecies and warnings. Our own time is pregnant with such events; and from all sides do we see the clouds gathering around the dark horizon; for only in the dark night do the evil-disposed come together and plan their nefarious and criminal designs. *Such a Satanic hot-bed of evil is Popery*, now making strides in all parts of the world, to regain the power which has been wrung from its hands—heedless as to the means by which it may accomplish its wicked ends. Among those means, we should not forget to number the Ecumenical Council called to the Babylonian city of seven hills. We doubt not but it may be of interest not only to candid and well-disposed Catholics (leaving aside the priest-ridden bigots), but also to every member of the dissenting churches and other differently believing communities, to learn something further *about the issue of that war which this largest and most Satanic institution on earth* (not unlike those who would assail Heaven in their rebellious designs, and unthrone God Almighty, the Creator and Lord of the universe) *began many centuries ago, in arrogance and wickedness.*

This and other urgent considerations of a high order have prompted us to make public these

Prophecies in regard to the downfall of Popery.

The following twenty-four magic figures were discovered as far back as four hundred and fifty years ago in the chartist cloister at Nuremberg (Bavaria); but not until a later period were they explained by Doctor Theophrastus Paracelsus, of Hohenheim. For those of our readers to whom the person of Doctor Paracelsus may be unknown, we subjoin the following short sketch of this extraordinary man, so hated by his cotemporaries and so wrongly judged even now.

Paracelsus (Philippus Aureolus Theophrastus) Bombast, called Von Hohenheim, was born at Einsiedeln, a small town near Zurich (Switzerland), in the year 1493. His father was a licentiate of medicine, and well versed in sciences. He educated his son with great care, and for his scientific instructions, he placed him under the charge of the celebrated Basilius Valentinus, one of the greatest alchemists of his time. Thus this extraordinary man, endowed as he was with very superior talents, flourished at a period in which the study of the God-like art of healing had been degraded into a scholastic squabble (just as it has been in this year 1869)—a period during which the disciples of Galen, through their shallowness and love for disputes, had become nothing better than miserable quacks.

Paracelsus being one of the greatest chemists of his time, soon became disgusted with the concoctions of medicines after the Galenic receipts. Experience too, taught him that the disciples of Galen had no success in any disease with their bleedings, purgatives and emetics (for therein consisted their whole apparatus); and that executioners, quacks and the like could boast of happier cures than the scholasts. He conceived the greatest hatred against the Galenic art, for he, a genius, could not follow their traditional doctrines. "I did," says Paracelsus, "embrace at the beginning these doctrines as my adversaries have done, but since I saw that from their procedures nothing resulted but death, murder, strangling, anchylosed limbs, paralysis, and so forth, that they held most diseases incurable, that they employed in all cases syrups, laxatives and the like, therefore have I quitted their wretched art, and sought for truth in any other direction. I asked myself, if there were no such thing as a teacher in medicine, where could I learn this art best?— no where better than in the open book of nature, written with God's finger. Through this door I entered—nature was my guide, and not a miserable apothecary's lamp."

Having subsequently traveled over the then known world, he spared neither pains nor industry to enlarge his mind with much useful knowledge. "I have followed the art," said he, "even to the danger of my life, and I have not been ashamed to learn from quacks, executioners and barbers." Provided with a rare treasure of wisdom and experience (extraordinary for his times) he was called to teach at the University at Basel (Switzerland). He made many enemies, particularly on account of the somewhat rough language with which he handled his adversaries. But his greatest enemies were his own pupils, to whom he did not divulge all his secrets, and the apothecaries, because his receipts were too plain. "These," he said, "are my enemies, because I do not help to empty their vials; my receipts do not consist of from forty to sixty ingredients, like those of the Galenic doctors; my duty, however, is not to help the apothecaries, but the sick."

In the high art of healing (of which, by the way, the physicians of our own day understand as much as a grave-digger about architecture), we look at him as a beacon, as a philosopher. Few have equalled him. He died at Salzburg (Austria), by the hand of an assassin.

In giving the explanations of the following figures, we have retained and in a measure imitated the *style* of the old German translations (the original being in Latin). We invite the reader to follow the description of these magic figures attentively. They are presented here in their antique shape and original rudeness.

Fig. I.

The First Figure.

The Pope is seen with two bears; into the mouth of one of them he pours down gold.

This figure presents to us the Pope and his clergy. He has abandoned himself to wickedness, pride and luxury. Who could gainsay that this is an ungodly life? nobody; but as it easily might be seen that there is nothing holy in him, he is cunning enough to gag the mouths of those who might find him out, in order to make them keep their peace; for the bears, which stand near him, signify those people who would feign tear him to pieces. But they open their mouths and swallow the gold. We see thus the whole clergy moulded after the Pope's fashion, and those who would not receive of his gifts cannot live; for not from among the popes does God choose the preachers of His Word, but from among others. Peter, the fisher, and Andrew, were not descendants from Caiaphas, nor from Annas; *nor will there arise a true prophet from among the popes.* The figure then signifies that not only the Pope, but all his friends and enemies also, are comprised within it, not seeking aid from the Holy Ghost, but stopping the mouths of the bears, and remaining indifferent.

Fig. II.

The Second Figure.

Here the Pope is represented with a cross, pushing his
staff down the throat of the eagle.

This signifies the Pope in the name of all the
clergy; the staff has a crook, the eagle is at the
feet of the Pope, who pushes the crook down his
throat. All comfort and hope of all the popes
come from the French; but as the emperor is
his master, he must try to use his cunning against
him. Like the wicked wife, who in order to avoid
the lashes of her husband, tries to overpower him
by means of her friends. The Pope likewise seeks
the aid of the French, who make the emperor
keep his peace, for he must yield lest war be
brought upon him. You must know, then, that
all those who are friendly to the Pope, act in such
a way that he who would be above him, is kept
down by them.

Fig. III.

The Third Figure.

**A Pope holding a banner is kneeling before a hand; a
fox hangs on to his coat.**

The explanation hereto is : the hand is the hand
of God. Now, there has been a Pope who repented and accused himself before God, who gives
him his blessing. Therefore we also see the banner behind him turning towards God. Now, there is
the fox behind him pulling his coat, the magic meaning of which is, that the self-same Pope is a fox in
his heart, giving good words to God. He is fasting,
and has quite a godly appearance, whilst he is full
of cunning. Magic would make us understand
that as he is looking towards God, and the fox
is behind him, the hand blesses him according to what is in his heart. The Pope has
meant to receive the true blessing, whilst God,
knowing all, has given him a blessing according
to his merits. The priestly order mean to do well
with mouth and knees, but they are, in fact, nothing more than foxes in priest's garb ; for the magic
meaning would make us believe that the fox may
still be seen in the garment. Christ has never
ordered it to be worn, nay, he compares one wearing it to a grave outwardly clean, but inwardly
rotten. The banner behind the Pope means
worldly power ; no apostle wore it ; the Pope,
however, being now so rich, requires cunning.

He commands in two realms—in the spiritual, by praying and kneeling; in the worldly, by cunning. Magic esteems every one sailing under the same colors a true servant of the devil.

Fig. IV.

The Fourth Figure.

We behold the Pope strangling an Eagle ; near him are some geese, roosters and a gray friar.

THE meaning of this figure is the arrogance of the priests in all things ; they strangle, through their Pope, the eagle which represents the Emperor ; and we see also geese and roosters which stand for lay brothers, to be strangled by the common priests. We find a report by means of the magic that common people are done away with, in another manner than that which the Pope uses against the Emperor ; for you must know that the Church of Rome will not be governed unto its end by the Emperor. He will not perish, nor his subjects, through the power of the Pope, but through false apostles and prophets. Take heed, therefore, not to turn away from God, cunning is too deeply rooted ; you would do well to keep your hearts clean and separated from your mouths. The trident in the Pope's hand, means the false power in the hands of the priesthood who boast of deriving it from the Trinity. The trident being turned downwards, means loss of power. The friar in the picture stands for all orders ; for since the times of Barbarossa, there has been *no monk who has done anything but cheating one as well as another.*

According to the decree of magic, you must not trust the monks, for they are the anti-Christ and false prophets arising from Popery. He will have

for himself the rabble, and rule with it, that is
with those who will rear roosters and geese, and
the Pope will lose his power over them ; the
eagle, however, he will strangle. The prophetic
monk will have for himself the common people.
Take care, therefore, of your conscience.

Fig. V.

The Fifth Figure.

The Pope on horseback, riding away; behind him a woman in a door.

A HOUSE has been built, and in its door-way stands a woman. Now, the Pope turns away from her, with a falcon on his hand. This means as follows : The house is the Church whereof the Pope is master. Riding away from it, signifies that he will never return. Since the Pope is master of the Church, he ought to stay in it, and not go away. As he goes hunting, we must consider him no longer its chief. Riding away from it, is a sign that he has lost his power over it ; it means also an expulsion. Any one has the right to capture him, for he has been banished from the Church. Now, if he is killed outside of it, he is no saint ; had he remained in the Church, he would have been sainted.

The woman in the doorway laments over his riding away. The beginning of the destruction of Churches is to be found in the fact that there is no one to guard them. Their power has gone. The woman predicts that his riding away will be the end of his Churches and of himself. She wants him to come back into the house of peace ; *but he turns to the world, lust and pride ; he abandons the Church, and this is the destruction of his realm, and the beginning of riot and discontent in the Churches.* As he holds a falcon instead of his key, and a horse instead of his mitre, we see the sibyl mourn over it. The cat not being at home, the mice can play. Being away from home, his household get in disorder and mutiny, and scorn him. On his return, he will find his house shattered and his dominion changed. This ride signifies that the good living of the Pope is the cause of heresy and its doctrines.

Fig. VI.

The Sixth Figure.

Here we see the Pope with his Key, and a menial striking him with a club.

THE cat being away, the mice dance. This is the cause of the riotous life of the Church. All the world is in uproar against it. All the meaning of it would be that there is a riot against the Church and the Pope, therefore he and his priests fly. The man with the club means the common man, the warrior, and all those who have been in opposition to priesthood. They make the Pope and the priests flee ; he, however, is not killed, for the Popes are not yet put aside ; they will remain ; they have stood the battle, and still retain the key. We read in this figure that those who chase him away, must risk their lives and lose them. The head at their feet, means that the one beating the Pope will lose his head. He who would punish others, must know whether he has the power to do so, and whether what he does is done conscientiously. However wicked the thief, and however well deserving his punishment, it does not free the executioner from the guilt of having shed blood. He who would undertake to be judge, must have a pure conscience.

The man with the club is a wanton ; it will be a wanton people who will execute the punishment. Although the punishment may not be wrong, the people will reap no benefit from it, for they will be judged as they have judged; cities, lords and others not excepted. He who would punish, must look into his own conscience, so that the punishment he has inflicted may not become his own. God will not overlook the executioner who puts the murderer to death.

Fig. VII.

The Seventh Figure.

Here we see the Pope with a lamb, wounding it with a sword; he has near him a naked monster, looking like a Pope, and a rod in the left hand, two keys in the right one.

THIS figure represents the sale of Christ, and the false faith in his blood; for we see the lamb killed with the sword that sticks out of the mouth of the Pope. He kills it with his mouth and sells it. The lamb means Christ. To spill his blood, means to live in riot and debauchery. The monster near it helps the Pope to hold the keys. This means a change in the sacrament, and that a new Pope has come; he acts with cunning, but he serves the blood of Christ falsely, and the heretics take hold of the sacraments, as the monster would make us believe. This Pope represents another Judas. We are given to understand that the sacrament will undergo great changes; the Holy Ghost will abandon it. The rod in the hand of the Pope is fresh and green; so will also be the punishment. The ancients having transmitted truth unto us, we ought to retain it. Look at the figures— the monster, the murderer, and the lamb! Take heed not to kill yourselves, nor to become monsters. There will be no true understanding of the flesh and blood of Christ, *unless the sects die out like the fig tree; then the Holy Ghost will come.*

Fig. VIII.

The Eighth Figure.

The Pope ruling over heaven, eagle and imperial crown.

WE see the falsehood of the Pope and his adherents in this picture. He points to heaven, as if he had power over it. The power in heaven, however, is not to be understood in the ordinary sense; he who would rule in it, must guide the flock on earth so as to lead them to it. The Pope understands it to be different; he thinks that having power over heaven, he can command also on earth. He affirms that he commands both in heaven and on earth; therefore we see the eagle and crown at his feet. This is entirely wrong. Neither is the earth nor heaven his, nor has he the command over the eagle and imperial crown. Know, therefore, that the figure stands for nothing else but for the *lying priesthood*. All the figures indicate the Pope's wickedness in lying; the magic hereto indicates the *lies of the Pope, and the boasting of possessing what does not belong to him, having no might nor right*.

Let us compare the dominion of the Pope to that of Christ, who says, "My kingdom is not of this world." The Popes assert that they possess power on earth too, which was not Christ's teaching. They would be like Mahommed, whose faith is based on riches, splendor, and power. Like unto him, they wish to subdue the emperor and world ; to elevate the religion of Christ that it may outshine all others. Thinking to command the world, they think also to spread the religion of Christ, not considering that He condemns them to hell with all their riches. Do not allow yourselves to be seduced, for no priest should possess the value of a farthing. Whatever it be, or howsoever small it be, it belongs to Satan—table, bed, bench, keys and all ; they should own nothing ; for having one farthing, they might claim more. As little as they can call heaven and earth their own, so little should a cent be called theirs. For Peter and James renounced all worldly possessions, and we cannot believe that they are God's. As long as they cling to worldly goods, we cannot look at them as apostles and successors of Christ.

Fig. IX.

The Ninth Figure.

OBSERVE in this figure the beginning of warning to the Pope, and of a period when his evil deeds excite public attention, and must be repented of and renounced. This is represented by the rooster at the hour of his crowing. This crowing announces to the Pope and his clergy that it is time to rise, as it did once awake Peter and the master of the house. The lamb being wounded in the neck, signifies that Christ has been wounded in His most sensitive place. A greater wound could not be inflicted on Him, for its head was separated from its body. Know, therefore, that the time is nigh. Christ has been martyred enough. The rooster crows.

The Pope has a bag filled to the brim with gold, so that he can hardly carry it. Pride then makes him cast away his staff, for the money occupies his mind fully. There is another meaning in this, namely, the clergy has arrived at its highest power, not only as regards riches, but also in cunning, subtleness and seduction, after the manner of the Pope and his heresy. This is the summit of their power, for never will they acquire a greater scope for their tricks, nor will their power for destruction become larger. You must know, also, that as the rooster has crowed, the hour is nigh, the beginning of the day. The sun is rising, and it is time to rise. Day and night are to be parted; the false power will fall. *Popery will be driven from the world, and a light will shine, not unlike that of the sun breaking forth after the night; and the time of joy for all the world shall dawn.* The Pope, the heretics, the preachers of heresy, who are false prophets, false apostles, will cease to exist. They will disappear like the night, with all their cunning, all their wisdom, and all their riches; and every one will walk in broad daylight, in the splendor of the sun.

Fig. X.

The Tenth Figure.

The Pope is standing in the crown, holding a razor in his hand. At his feet is a wolf with a sword.

THE wolf here appears to attack Popery. He grasps his sword, and with it power and dominion. Magic gives us to believe that these wolves are of the scorpion species; for the wolf represents the peasants, who will be the first to attack. The razor in the Pope's hand attests his consecration. The consecration of the Pope and all the clergy may be likened to a razor. The razor in his hand is the emblem of power, and by losing it he loses his power, and is no more than any other mortal. God never intended to place heavenly power at the discretion of the Pope. The Pope standing in the crown, and not on it, means that he is like a king in his realm, defended on all sides. The peasants will be the first to drive him from his stronghold; the sword will be wrested from him, and the razor with which he had shorn others, will be turned against him and his adherents. Magic gives us to understand that the crown comprises all his dominion, and the clergy over which he rules. Although he appears to be strong in his dominion, it will be wrested from him, like the crown, the sword, the keys, and the razor. The downfall of Romanism and the Church is at hand. The wolves will tear them to pieces, *particularly those who belong to his caste.* However, this is only the first attack against him and his adherents; his power will be weakened, but not quite annihilated. The wolf, so magic tells us, stands here for a priest, and wolves will attack him. He has consecrated them, and they will turn against him.

Fig. XI.

The Eleventh Figure.

Here stands the Pope, holding two keys in one hand, up-
lifted by an angel ; in the other hand he holds a
rod ; at his feet a peacock, with the tail
spread out.

THE former figure indicated the loss of the
sword, which would fall into the hands of the
wolves. As we know already that in the magic
language wolves stand for priests, we must believe
that they will be the ones to make an attack, and
hold the power, which in their turn they will lose.
God will send an angel to take the power from them,
and after its loss they will no longer be able to
bind and unbind. The confidence placed in them
will be lost, as well as the immunities of Popery.
No one should then be led to believe *that the
power of Popery will be everlasting.* We read it
in all magic and in all constellations.

The Pope will lose all his power little by little,
and like a tree that is withered, will be cut down,
for the dry rod in his hand shows *his decline and
rapid fall.* That which grows suddenly, also
perishes suddenly ; but it is not so here, for we
read in the Word of God that the fig tree suddenly
dried up and grew no more. The rod signifying
punishment, would indicate that he carries his punishment in his own hand, like an unruly pupil who
is punished by his schoolmaster. The peacock which
appears to gladden his sight, indicates that the

Pope will appeal to *Austria, and that she will give him help.* Magic says that a peacock is a merry bird, the emblem of Austria, and is at the side of the Pope to sustain him. Notwithstanding the punishment to which the Pope will be subjected, he will be upheld by Austria. The angel lifting up the keys, is a sure sign that *the grace of God has departed from the Pope. None of those who assist him will be saved. Timely circumstances will help him, but he will not be helped by God.*

Fig. XII.

The Twelfth Figure.

Here is the Pope with a Pilgrim's staff, and before him a Man in armor, with bloody swords and spears.

The last two figures represented the misfortune and downfall of the Pope, through the Wolf and the Angel—the third misfortune he will receive at the hands of warriors. The Pope will become a pilgrim and a stranger in Rome. The iron-clad man indicates that he will be driven from his seat by war; but the warrior will not attempt to take the life of the Pope. Though death is threatening him, the hand which is outstretched from the clouds turns the wrath of the warrior away, the punishment of being driven from the seat is enough for the present. So anxious is the man to take away the Pope's life, that he wrathfully wounds himself by grasping violently the sharp edge of the sword. The wrath of the Lord is soothed. Swords and spears mean war, rebels and multitudes of warriors. The stars signify that the hand of the Lord turns the sword away, that the Pope may not entirely perish; for, all that happens to us on earth, is decreed in heaven. Although that magic would make us believe that the end of the Pope is at hand, the decree of God is different; He breaks the power of the Pope's adversaries, so that he may have the opportunity of reforming; for God is very lenient; it is long before he punishes the wicked.

This is the third in the series of the trials inflicted on the Pope. We see him now driven from his home. Harken, ye most obstinate of the Popes! What else but luxury is meant to be driven away—for luxury is at the bottom of all this trial. What is the Pope to be punished for? For his fasting, his praying and confession? No! But for his falsehood. God in his kindness will not as yet deprive him of his office.

Fig. XIII.

The Thirteenth Figure.

The Pope surrounded and attacked by three bears, two at his sides and one on his head.

THE decree of God being passed, another punishment follows. The bears attack the Pope and will ultimately swallow him. One will take hold of his head, that is to say, the Pope will be oppressed by the raging bears and torn to pieces by them. The three bears signify *that the faith will be divided into three parts.* Three new faiths will arise. And as the bears feed on prey, so will the Pope be torn to pieces and devoured. The three creeds will not occupy the office of the Pope as they hoped to do; one, however, will. The bears doing away with the Pope are like dogs attacking a man; they do not become angels, but remain bears. These, and not angels, make the attack. Magic tells us that the bears stand for men who live on spoils; they devour out of envy, hatred and avarice. From their nature we are led to believe that devils, and not angels, will cause the ruin of the Pope. His own followers will attack him so terribly that he will not find any comfort in his book; all that will be left him, is to own himself to be a liar and a cheat. The bears will perish as bears do perish. *After* *the Pope and the bears shall have perished, the Millennium will begin and the true understanding of faith, love and hope.**

---

*That will be *the New Church, the New Jerusalem.* —[REMARK OF THE EDITOR.]

Fig. XIV.

The Fourteenth Figure.

The Pope is seen with a banner in his hand. A dove and a serpent, speaking to each other, are seen at his side.

This picture indicates the *arrogance of the Pope.* Although the punishment mentioned in the preceding figure—the bears eating his flesh—shall take place, the Pope nevertheless will continue to be arrogant. The serpent signifies the devil Leviathan, and the dove the Holy Ghost or the voice of God. They are having an altercation; the Pope, bearing a banner, is looking on to see the Holy Ghost fighting against the devil. He bids the devil to quit the earth; against which the latter is combatting. The Pope then turns away from both, and says in his wicked heart: the banner is mine, that is Rome, and all the followers of the Romish Church. Mine also is power and the world. I have no need of you; I have already reaped my harvest; I have fattened my sow; do as you please; I have my share. And he turns away from them in the belief that he no longer needs them. We see herein his arrogance and *proud haughtiness,* which he does not relinquish. *Neither the devil nor the Lord, so he thinks, have anything to do with him, he is his own master.* He also imagines that no one can deprive him of what he holds from Peter and Paul; that he needs neither of them any longer. Having the power in his own hand, he believes himself to be able to rule. The devil, if he should need him, would be *at his command too, and would obey him*. He continues to be sinful and arrogant, and grows in wickedness. He does not heed the punishments that are inflicted on him, one after another, and those which are to come yet; but he boasts of the freedom of his banner, and of his book. The Word being eternal, he believes that he will hold the keys too forever. No one can take them from him; but, like Judas, who was an Apostle chosen by Christ, and was still a traitor, so will the apostolic power be taken from the Pope and another be placed in his stead.

Fig. XV.

The Fifteenth Figure.

The Pope wearing his tiara, which is pushed down by a unicorn. A man, confessing his sins, kneels before him, and he absolves him.

THERE is no end to the plagues yet; many more will come up, for the Pope relies too much on his own power. This figure indicates that the Pope will be deprived of his power of absolving sins, of binding on earth and in heaven, and all this on account of his whoredom. The unicorn being a very clean animal; has such a sharp scent that it discerns a virgin; this animal stands for God, who knows all. The unicorn, which is seen pushing down the tiara of the Pope, is a sign of his degradation. His office and all his appurtenances will be taken away from him. This is the following plague, and almost the last, which God has decreed. God takes away all his freedom and all his comfort; he is like a dishonest captain, who is deprived of his office and becomes an executioner. *The Pope will be dethroned, his tiara taken from him, and his power will never return to his followers and name.* All the fruit of the tree, that is to say the priesthood, will also be deprived of its power, and the tree will wither. *Like the weed which is torn up and cast into the fire, will this evil be uprooted and also be cast into the fire.* That will be their last judgment-day—their downfall and condemnation. But it will not be the judgment-day of the blessed ; for after this day another will come, and all the inhabitants of the earth will rejoice and live in peace. The fruits of the tree will no longer pollute the earth ; the devil, in the shape of the serpent, will be cast into the fire of the lowest hell. The Man on earth will be guilty of no heresies ; no false apostles will appear to him, and no false Christians shall there be.

Fig. XVI.

The Sixteenth Figure.

There stands a Monk; in one hand he holds a rose, in the other a sickle. On one side a fire-poker, and on the other a naked thigh.

This figure has the following meaning. Like the rose which smells sweet in May and rejoices every one, whilst it withers in the fall and nothing remains but the barren bush, so will this Monk be sweet to the people. The multitude will run to hear him; but a time of drought will follow, nothing will remain but the barren bush; that is, empty words without flavor and taste. The sickle means that as every thing is hewn down with it, plants and weeds, so will good and evil be cut down and cast into the fire. This is indicated by the poker. The naked thigh shows that there will be a great uncovering of whoring, so great that all hearts will be laid bare, and whores and whoremongers will be known. All evil deeds will be uncovered: the naked thigh is the wickedest and the most far-spread whoredom ever known. The Monk shows that there will arise a man who will be listened to with great admiration by the multitude; but his autumn will come too, and he will wither. He will cut down all that is good and evil. He will spare nothing, and inflict much trouble. His autumn will be like a fire, in which he will be consumed like wood. The instruments

at his feet indicate that he cannot escape, for they
surround him on all sides.   After his mission shall
be fulfilled with the upper signs, he passes on to
the lower—the reign of whoredom and the consuming by fire.   In this manner will be consumed
all the good he has done.

Fig. XVII.

The Seventeenth Figure.

The Emperor and Empress behind a curtain; before it the Pope, at whose feet lies an ox.

THE Pope will receive help from the ox in his undertakings, and protection in need; but the work will be so difficult that the ox will grow tired to exhaustion, and lie down at the Pope's feet, and will be killed. Magic shows that the ox means the Swiss, the Pope's guard, who will fight for him; but they exhaust themselves in their efforts, and they will be of no avail to him; that is to say, that the Pope will loose his power, and great distress will come unto him. The Emperor and his wife behind the curtain shows that Popery will be raised again, for the peacock (Austria) means well with the Pope, and will continue to do so. Know, then, that although the destruction of the Popish realm has been predicted, the Emperor will continue in his belief in the power of the Pope to open heaven. This will mislead the Emperor, and thereby the Pope will rise again with the hope that his power, his honor, authority and riches will still remain. The Pope and the ox will succumb; another will take the power, but the Emperor will restore him. This, however, will not be of any duration, for the tiara has been taken from him by God, angels have deprived him of his keys, the warrior has attacked him with the sword, etc. Nothing will be of avail; nay, the empire will find its ruin in it; and there will be no increase, but rather decrease and loss. With the growing idolatry the empire will decay. *The higher the power of the Pope rises, the deeper will the empire sink.* The Pope will arise, but not the ox, which will be too much exhausted.

Fig. XVIII.

The Eighteenth Figure.

We see the Pope standing upright, and a she-bear leans upon him, surrounded by young cubs sucking her.

AFTER the downfall of the Pope and the ox, there will come a time when the Pope will grow hungry, like the young cubs. This visitation will be one of the last. The poverty and hunger will be the sign that *the end of his dominion approaches.* God having withdrawn his hand, who is the Emperor that would protect and support the Pope? None. He is fallen from the grace of God; he has been doomed to misery, and he will suck his claws like a bear. Poverty will open his eyes. His last hour will come. He will grow wild like a she-bear deprived of milk for her cubs. She tears down every thing in her rage. This will be the fate of the Pope and his priests. But they will struggle to the last; for riches and power being given up, the evil survives in the heart, and brings forth rage and excommunications; therefore he is like a wild she-bear, which is more furious than the male. Empires deprived of the grace of God fall to atoms, not by any righteous man, but they destroy one another. Like a city where there is no unity nor security, one devours the other. Cities falling through their own iniquity, *not through the power of tyrants, but by combatting against each other. No pious man will have a hand in the Pope's destruction, for he will perish through his own priesthood.*

Fig. XIX.

The Ninteenth Figure.

The Pope, before him a fox holding the Pope's banner and keys in his mouth.

This figure shows the approaching end of Popery. The fox is one of the Pope's own household and tribe, *for all that the Pope does he is doing with the cunning of a fox.* The heretics are the fox, who will carry away the Pope's banner, and this will be the end of him. He retains neither keys nor banner, neither cities nor land, neither empire nor dukedom; he is an outcast. His own foxes have driven him away with cunning. Through the heretics Popery will see its end, and this is the last of his number and tribe. Although many heretics have risen previously, nothing has been done to him; but there have been many of them, and such a constellation has never before appeared; but the rabble grows furious and is great, and the executioners are ready.

Fig. XX.

The Twentieth Figure.

There is a naked Priest sitting, and a peasant near him, and a box with money.

WHO could possess less than nakedness and be deprived of all? But the priesthood will be naked and deprived of all. None of them will know where to direct their steps, and the poorest peasant will be richer than they. *This is the destruction of the Pope and his final deposition.* He, the Pope, will be destroyed, and with him all his cardinals, patriarchs, bishops, orders, priests, and all—all will be consumed, and finally also the heretics.

They must all come to an end who live after the manner of the Priests, who have been anointed; they all will go down, one alone will remain, the others will disappear like snow. Many wonderful events will come to pass before the Pope will sit naked on a hard stone.

Fig. XXI.

The Twenty-first Figure.

There stands the Pope with his tiara off, giving it to sheep lying at his feet.

THERE will again be a Pope, but he will be pure and glorious, after the manner of Peter and Paul. His arrogance will be laid aside. His pride, too, his avarice and his overbearing power. He will be meek after the fashion of the Apostles, and the sheep lying at his feet will not be merchants, nor usurers, nor lawyers. Nor will they be adulterers, nor thieves, nor blasphemers, nor whoremongers, nor murderers, nor heretics. But the lives of the people will be unspotted and pure as the life of a lamb. And the Pope will radiate forth harmony and heavenly peace : these also will pervade his whole flock. And thus also the following figures signify : *purity of heart of the Pope and his flock.*

Fig. XXII.

The Twenty-second Figure.

Therein kneels a Priest, on whom an Angel puts a hat.

Know then, that not by man, but by the angels
of God, shall the Pope be crowned. For all those
who have been crowned by man shall perish like
a tree that has been condemned by God. Mankind shall have a Pope not after the fashion of his
own laws, nor after that of the peasants and heretics,
but after the will of God. The Pope (shepherd) shall
again possess power by the grace of God, and he
shall rule in the spirit of mercy and love of God.
No one shall be allowed to say, make the Pope
after my fashion, nor shall the choice of him be in
the power of mortals; and none will be elected
by the judgments of men, which are all false and
worthless; and thus every thing effected by such
elections is likewise false and idolatrous. But
God will choose him, for he has chosen the first,
and so shall he do the last, for His is the privilege
and power, not man's. For if men could choose
the Pope, it would be as it was before, the devil
would be among them; for he is friendly to all
such elections by self-directed men.

Fig. XXIII.

The Twenty-third Figure.

The Pope sitting in a chair, whilst Angels are holding a curtain around him.

THE true Mass will be celebrated once more, the false ones having been set aside by the Pope with the razor, by heretics who break up his dominion. This Mass will be instituted by God, and not by men. The heretics having died, there will be no interference on their part. The Pope will then derive his power from God. Angels placing him in a chair and holding a curtain around him, give us to understand *that the Pope will be put on his throne by angels, and not by men; his power likewise will emanate from God, and not from men.* What could be more becoming than the garments laid on him by the hand of angels, or the throne prepared for him by their hands, and not by those of men; for his best ornament will be his following in the footsteps of Christ and his apostles. He will restore to life those who are dead; he will heal the sick; the blind will see again; and the leprous will be cleansed. This will be the garments of angels— *that by his virtues he will shine, praising God the Father in heaven, who gave them to him.*

Fig. XXIV.

The Twenty-fourth Figure.

Here the Pope places his hat on a lamb with seven horns.

This is the end, and signifies: the lamb with seven horns being Christ, the Pope will crown him, and thereby confess that *Christ, and not a man, is Pope ; that Christ's is the power, and not man's ; for the Pope on earth is to be a perfect (regenerated) man, teaching his flock by his example how to live in Christ.*

Thus all will be united under his power; there will be no discord, but *there will be one shepherd, even Christ, over the seven races of man.* Under his rule we shall then remain for ever. Satan will no longer have any power over us; through all eternity we shall live and be full of joy and gladness. But all false Christians will have died, as well as all false apostles and false prophets. *The heretics and unbelievers too will have died ;* for their gods having perished, they must needs perish likewise. But hard and difficult will it be for us to reach this goal; many fountains will dry up, and many changes take place, before that time arrives. Before this comes to pass, however, *there will perish all usurers, all the rich, and all the children and princes of this world ; they will perish like a rabble, and be consumed, and all vice and wickedness will have disappeared from the pathway of the godly.*

Now, at the conclusion of these magic figures, we find it necessary, dear reader, to add a few explanatory remarks, without which the end of Popery might remain unintelligible.

More than four hundred and fifty years have elapsed since the discovery of these magic figures. It will be easily perceived that the explanations given by Paracelsus are all brief and pointed. Every attentive reader will have observed that the greater part of these prophecies have been fulfilled with wonderful precision; he will see to what extent this has been the case; yet he may possibly entertain some doubt, as Popery appears, according to the last three figures, to have no end.

The end of Popery, with all its power, both temporal and spiritual, and all its satanic influences, is given in the twentieth figure. In the time therein predicted, Popery, and with it *the Catholic Church, will come to an end.* For, with its abominable adoration of saints, and its so-called divine service, the Catholic Church presents rather the appearance of a heathen than of a Christian worship. How would Christ have appeared in his entrance into Jerusalem, riding on an ass's colt, had he been adorned with the hat of a Pagan bishop of our day, or with the tiara of a Pope!

Thus will disappear the Catholic Church, which is already dead spiritually. The 21st, 22d, 23d, and 24th Figures show forth *a new state of the Church.* In it there will be no Pope; for *the Lord will be the Pope, living amidst His people,* as we read in the Revelation of St. John (chap. 21): "*Behold the tabernacle of God is with men, and he will dwell with them, and they shall be his people, and God himself shall be with them, and be their God. And God shall wipe away all tears from their eyes; and there shall be no more death, neither sorrow nor crying, neither shall there be any more pain: for the former things are passed away.* (Rev. chap. 21 v. 1–4.) *And there shall be no night there; and they need no candle, neither light of the sun: for the Lord God giveth them light; and they shall reign for ever and ever.* (Rev. chap. 22 v. 5.)

Nor will there be any earthly Pope (in the former or present sense of that word), *but the Lamb will be the Pope,* as it is written in Revelation, where we read: " *And there shall be no more curse; but the throne of God and of the Lamb shall be in it, and his servants shall serve him.*" (Rev. chap. 22 v. 3.) This new state of the Church on earth will be

𝕿𝖍𝖊 𝖓𝖊𝖜 𝕮𝖍𝖚𝖗𝖈𝖍, 𝖔𝖗 𝖙𝖍𝖊 𝕹𝖊𝖜 𝕵𝖊𝖗𝖚𝖘𝖆𝖑𝖊𝖒,

as it has been revealed by Isaiah (chap. 65 v. 17): " For behold, I create new heavens and a new earth: and the former shall not be remembered, nor come into mind." Thus too it is written in the Revelation (chap. 21, 22.)

The following explanations may serve for a better understanding of the new Church, called the " New Jerusalem." From the creation of the world down to our own time, there have existed in succession *four* distinct *Churches* on our globe.

One before the deluge, which is called the *Adamic* Church; this was followed by the *Noetic* Church (that of Noah and his posterity); then came the *Israelitic*, and finally the *Christian* Church, which latter has now but an external existence. These four Churches are described by Daniel (chap. 2, 31–43), when he relates how he saw the statue of Nebuchadnezzar in his dream; and in chapter 7, verses 3 to 9, when he speaks of the four beasts arising from the earth. In each of the four churches, four different changes took place. The first of these changes represented the appearing of the Lord Jehovah, and the redemption of man; this was the morning or beginning of a Church; the second change represented its teaching, and thereby its day or progressive stage. Then the third change, its decline or evening; and finally, the fourth, the night, end or termination of a Church. After the end of each Church, the Lord Jehovah comes to sit in judgment over the adherents or followers of that church which has passed away; and to separate the good from the wicked. The former he elevates into heaven, while he condemns the latter to hell. *

---

* When we speak of a *hell*, dear reader, you must not think of the hell that has been invented by imbecile Catholic priests, and which they have peopled with personal devils and Satans—a place where the souls of the departed have to undergo all the tortures of the Inquisition, and are thus tormented in virtue of Papal authority. But, in its true sense, hell is a place of banishment for the souls of the deceased, who have neither any goodness nor any truth in themselves, nor any capability of receiving the same, owing to their own perverse and wicked will. Thus *there are no personal devils, or Satans*, for *devil* in the spiritual sense denotes the evils of hell; while by *Satan* are designated the falsities of hell, both in contradistinction heavenly good and heavenly truth.

With those gathered around him, the Lord Jehovah forms the *new Heaven*, whereas the wicked
constitute the *new Hell*.

From this *new Heaven*, the Lord Jehovah brings
down "THE NEW CHURCH," or "THE NEW JERU-
SALEM," of which St. John says (chap. 21, v. 2):
"And I saw the Holy City, the new Jerusalem,
coming down from God out of heaven, prepared
as a bride adorned for her husband." But this is
done by means of the revelation of truths from
His mouth, or by His Word, and through Inspiration. Both these divine operations united, are at
the same time called "Redemption." Without
the latter, it is impossible for man to be regenerated and saved. Each of the first three Churches,
after losing its spiritual vitality, has passed away,
and been swallowed up by the next in succession.
Thus the first or Adamic Church, which is to be
considered as the *primitive Church*, existed
before the deluge, by which its end or termination
is allegorically described. The second, or Noctic
Church, which is also called the *ancient Church*,
flourished chiefly in Asia, and to a less extent in
Africa. It was desecrated through the worship of
idols, and thus came to an end. The third—the
Jewish or Israelitic Church—commenced with the
proclamation of the ten Commandments on Mount
Sinai. It continued as long as the Word of God,
written down by Moses and the Prophets, was
faithfully observed, and until a profane disregard of
the same, when that Church also perished. This
event took place at the time of the advent of the
Lord himself, who is the Word, and who was

nailed to the cross. The fourth is that which exists in our own times, viz., the *Christian Church*. It has already outlived itself spiritually, and is near its end. For the end of a Church, and the consummation of its time, have come when it has no longer any genuine truth or any genuine good left; when consequently both what is good and what is true have ceased to exist in it, so that in their stead evils and falsities have begun to reign. Then, nothing remains but uncertainty as to the existence of God, as to heaven and hell, and a life after death (an unbelief which we find now actually prevailing everywhere.) All those who have become confirmed in the denial of a God, and all those who float in uncertainty between denying and affirming, actually shun the light, and flee away from it into darkness. If they are ordained priests, they have a false and deceptive light in regard to all these things, and thus are like owls, cats and mice in the darkness of night.

The end of those four Churches rendered the institution of a *fifth* Church necessary. The necessity of the latter is obvious, from the fact that in creating the world, the Lord had no other object in view than to provide a constant conjunction between Himself and mankind, so that man might live in Him, and He in man. From this may be inferred the principal condition for the permanent existence of each of these Churches, namely, the *knowledge* and *acknowledgment of a God, with whom each and every one might become conjoined.* This fundamental condition has, however, not been fulfilled by the first four Churches. For in the primitive Church, which existed before the deluge, they worshipped an *invisible God*, with whom no conjunction is possible. The same was the case with the ancient Church, which came after the deluge. In the Israelitic Church, they worshipped Jehovah, who is invisible in Himself, (Exodus 33, v. 18–23), but under a human form. For we see Him assuming the form of an angel, and appearing thus to Moses, Abraham, Sarah, Hagar, Gideon, Joshua, and to the Prophets. This appearance, however, under human form was but a *prefiguration* of the Lord that was to come. Therefore also must the whole as well as the details and particulars of the preceding Churches, be looked upon as prefigurative and typical.

The fourth Church, however, which was called Christian, did at least orally and externally profess to believe in *one only* God, *in three persons*, each of which is looked upon as God himself—a Trinity divided asunder and not united in one person. They were obliged to believe in God the Father, God the Son, and God the Holy Ghost, each one of whom is invisible. Nevertheless, this one and invisible God has come into the world under a *human form*, not only for the sake of saving mankind, but also to become visible and conjoined to men.

Daniel, explaining the Dream of Nebuchadnezzar, in speaking of the four empires, means the four churches; and predicts that a *fifth*, or *new church* should follow, surpassing in splendor and in glory all the churches that had preceded, and vanished away in succession. He says (chap. ii.

v. 44), "In the days of these kings shall the God of heaven set up a kingdom which shall never be destroyed ; and the kingdom shall not be left unto other people, but it shall break in pieces and consume all these kingdoms, and it shall stand forever." This fifth, new and last church has been revealed by the Lord himself, who, in His infinite mercy, disclosed its first or initiatory doctrines more than a hundred years ago, through a servant especially chosen and sanctified by Him. *This church was thereafter, in reality, established by Him in the year* 1838, *in one of the great cities of Eastern Europe, and thus also began to exist externally and naturally.* But, in that land of Herod, persecutions at once commenced, and the new-born infant (the new church) was compelled to flee to Egypt. There it must remain hidden, that it may grow and acquire strength, until the servants of Herod shall have become powerless, and the child be able to return in safety to Nazareth. We must add that, *in this fifth, new and last church, all other churches, creeds and systems of religion, without any exception, will be merged and swallowed up forever.*

For the reader who is not acquainted with the nature of this new dispensation, it must be of interest to learn at least THE FUNDAMENTAL TENETS AND GENERAL PRINCIPLES OF :

The New Church, called the New Jerusalem.

(DANIEL, chap. vii., v. 12—13) and (REVELATION, chap. xxi. and xxii.)

The Heavenly Doctrines of the New Jerusalem are the following, viz :

I. JEHOVAH GOD is the Creator and Preserver of Heaven and Earth. He is essential Love and essential Wisdom, or Good itself and Truth itself. He is *one* in essence as well as in person ; but in Him there is a Divine Trinity, consisting of Father, Son and Holy Ghost; as in man—Soul, Body and vital manifestation form but one being. The Lord and Saviour Jesus Christ is this God.

II. Jehovah God as *the* Divine Truth, which is the Word, has (without, however, separating the Divine Good from himself,) descended to us and assumed human nature, in order to subjugate the Powers of Darkness and destroy their influence ; to reduce the Spiritual World to a normal condition ; to prepare on Earth the way for a New Church, and thereby to accomplish the great work of Redemption. Through suffering and temptation He has glorified His humanity, by fully uniting it to His indwelling Divinity. All those will be saved who sincerely believe in Him, and have received this faith in their hearts as well as their minds, and who manifest it in their entire life.

III. The Word of the Lord, or the Sacred Scripture, was written by Divine Inspiration. It contains a threefold sense, or a heavenly, spiritual and natural meaning. These three meanings are intimately connected with each other by correspondence. In all these senses it contains Divine Truth adapted, in their several degrees, to the Angels of the three Heavens, as well as to Man on

Earth. As the Lord and His Word are one, and as by the Word man is conjoined with Heaven, it is of the highest importance that we should discern the genuine, Divinely-inspired Books of the Word from all other writings. Those Books which form the perfect and complete Canon of the Sacred Scripture, and are known as such, are the following: In the Old Covenant—the Five Books of Moses, called Genesis, Exodus, Leviticus, Numbers, Deuteronomy, the Book of Joshua, the Book of Judges, the two Books of Samuel, the two Books of Kings, the Psalms of David; the Prophets—Isaiah, Jeremiah, (with the Lamentations,) Ezekiel, Daniel, Hosea, Joel, Amos, Obadiah, Jonah, Micah, Nahum, Habakbuk, Zephaniah, Haggai, Zacharias, and Malachi. And in the New Covenant, the Four Evangelists—Matthew, Mark, Luke, and John, and the Revelation of John, or the Apocalypse.

IV. All that is evil, be it of the inclination or thought, or of the life, is to be shunned as a sin against God, and as coming from the Devil, that is from Hell,—destroying in man all capacity for enjoying the bliss of Heaven. On the contrary, all that is good,—good inclinations, good thoughts, good actions, ought to be cherished and loved, as being divine and emanating from God. Every act of love and charity, of justice and righteousness,—towards society in general, and individuals in particular,—ought to be done by man as if from himself, with the express acknowledgment, however, that in reality it is done by the Lord, who works in and through man.

V. Immediately after the death of the material body (*which is never thereafter assumed again,*) man rises to a new life, in virtue of his spiritual and substantial body. He thus continues to live in a perfect human form, with all his former faculties of mind and body unimpaired. Hence, death is but the transfer from the natural to the spiritual world, and a continuation of life, which will be either eternally happy or unhappy, according to the ruling love which man has acquired while living on earth ; and which is in conformity with the divine truths of the Holy Word, or with their opposites, for, every man is adjudged individually after death, either for Heaven or Hell, according to what his life has been in the body, either good or evil.

VI. Concerning *children* who die before they have attained their full powers of mind and reached the age of mature judgment,—be they baptized or unbaptized, be they in the Christian Church or not, be they born of godly or ungodly parents,—they will *all* be received by the Lord into Heaven, and after they have been instructed and their understandings developed, they will become partakers of the bliss and perfection of Angels.

VII. Through the mercy and providence of God, the proper means of salvation are rendered accessible to all mankind, so that men of every creed or denomination on earth, be they Jews, Christians, Mahommetans, or Heathen, may be saved, provided they live in love and charity towards one another from religious motives, and in accordance with the knowledge and understanding they possess. Nevertheless, the New and true Christian Religion, inasmuch as it derives its existence directly from our Lord and Saviour Jesus Christ,—who is the only God of Heaven and Earth,—is of all creeds the best adapted to effect a firm and complete union or conjunction with Him; therefore, it should be considered more excellent, heavenly and divine than any other religion.

VIII. All the circumstances and all the occurrences of human life, be they productive of happiness or unhappiness, stand under the direct and immediate care of Divine Providence. Nothing can occur or happen to man,—either in general or in particular,—which, in its most minute details, as well as in its totality, is not calculated to promote his eternal welfare in a manner only known to Infinite Wisdom.

IX. *True conjugial Love*, which can exist only between one man and one woman, constitutes one of the *fundamental characteristics* of the *New Church;* for it is founded on the marriage or intimate union between Goodness and Truth, and necessarily corresponds to the marriage of the Lord with His Church. Hence, it is more heavenly, more spiritual, more holy, more pure, and more innocent than any other love among angels or men.

X. Man has not Life in himself; he is only the recipient of Life from the Lord, who alone has Life in Himself. This Life is communicated by an influx from the Lord into all and everything in the spiritual world; be it in Heaven or in Hell, or in the intermediate state, called the World of Spirits,—and also into everything in the natural world; but it is received by each one differently, according to the quality of the recipient.

XI. *The last judgment*, of which mention is so often made in the Gospels and the Apocalypse, —consists of a separation of the good from the wicked in the spiritual world, where they had lived congregating and mingling with one another freely, ever since the first advent of the Lord, and had thus continued until His second coming. The last judgment did thus actually take place (as a *spiritual* event) in the year 1757, when, according to Scripture, the first Heaven and Earth (the old Church) came to an end, and the foundation for a New Church was laid, in which everything will be made new.

XII. As an act of the mercy of God to mankind, who, without it, would have been swallowed up in eternal death,—*the second advent of the Lord has already taken place, and is still taking place up to the present day; for, it is a coming not in person, but in the power and glory of the spiritual sense of His Holy Word, which is Himself. Hence, the Holy City, the New Jerusalem, is even now descending from God; it comes down from Heaven as a bride adorned for her husband.*

DEAR READER!—Should you ever hear of such a *New Church*, beware of following the wrong track; for, there exist not only here in America, but also in Europe, a number of societies and congregations, the members of which style themselves members of the "New Church." They actually imagine themselves to be already in the New Church, and thus believe that when they die they will find an appointed place ready, waiting for them in the Holy City, in the midst of the New Jerusalem !

They build houses wherein to assemble, and to worship after their own fashion, putting, as it were, the Lord God to death ; and because they are too indifferent to read the doctrines of the New Church for themselves, they appoint a priest, who expounds the doctrines to them, so that they may be spared the labor of thinking ;—just as the practice was in the by-gone old Churches. They also keep the holy Sabbath, although they should know better and understand what Sabbath means. They hold their idolatrous worship and are baptized by their ordained priest. From his polluted hands they receive their Holy Communion. In their praying and singing they would fain outdo any old Catholic Nun, as is still the custom in the old Churches, and they flatten their noses against their hands, and call this " awakening devotion." They build Theological Seminaries with the money which is donated to them, and *which they ought to employ for the benefit of their poor brethren.* But these seminaries—theological barracks—are for young idlers and loiterers, who shrink from following an honest calling, and rather prefer to be fed by the sacrifices of others, so that they may afterwards become expounders of the New Church doctrines. These doctrines were given by the

Lord Himself, and are very plain, clear and easily understood! Nevertheless, those priests expound them after their own preconceived ideas and erroneous notions, and mix them up with their own false and pernicious doctrines. And nonsense, which they themselves have originated, is served up to their flock as the food of angels. Thus they endeavor to elucidate the fundamental tenets or rudiments of the New Church (for these are all they possess,) as if the Sun of the Lord had need to be illuminated by a dirty tallow candle of lazy, arrogant, audacious Pharisees! Such a house they call their church or temple, forgetting that the Lord has said: "The Heaven is my throne and the Earth is my footstool, where is the house that ye build unto me? and where is the place of my rest?" (Isaiah lxvi. v. 1.) And: "The Most High dwelleth not in temples made with hands." "The hour cometh, when ye shall neither in this mountain nor yet at Jerusalem worship the Father —they that worship Him must worship Him in spirit and in truth." (John, chap. iv. v. 21–24.)

Such new Churches, and their impure worship, are represented in the spiritual world of heaven by *an old house, built of rotten wood, over a filthy swamp, from which arises a putrid stench; surrounded with a railing of new wood, the whole structure painted over with the colors of the new Church. Thence arises the fetid smell of putrid horse urine, as incense for the worship which is celebrated in it !*

The *new Church,* called the *New Jerusalem,* was first established spiritually by the *Lord Himself,* through *revelations.* *He Himself* laid the foundation of it on earth *naturally* through *revelations.**

With what right then do these intruders ordain themselves as *priests of the Lord?* Who has given them such an order? From whom do they hold their commission? The *Lord Himself* is the Architect of the new Church on earth; the *Lord Himself* selects His builder and His workmen; *He Himself* baptizes those who are elected by *Him* to be members of the new Church, and the *Lord Himself* holds communion with His children in the new Church.†

You must first become meek and humble, ye arrogant, self-created idols. Learn some honest trade! You should first seek truth! Clear *your own* field, and till *your own* ground, in order that you may be able to sow the Lord's wheat, provided you receive such, on a field given to you by Him. Then, and then only, when the fruit has grown under the blessed hand of the Lord, may you go and feed the hungry!

Therefore, dear reader, should you hear any rumors and noise about *new Churches*, and should see that *any visible or external worship* is cele-

---

* Already Swedenborg has expressed himself in the following manner in regard to the new Church: "The Church which succeeded those three is the (Christian) Church, which is an internal Church, differing from the Jewish as the light of the moon from a dark night. But because this Church has come to its end by the accomplishment of the last judgment, a new Church, which is called the New Jerusalem in the Apocalypse, *will* now be instituted from the Lord, *to which the things which are at this day published by me will be subservient.* IT WILL BE INSTITUTED ALSO ELSEWHERE."

† "*But I say unto you, I will not drink henceforth of this fruit of the vine, until that day when I drink it* NEW *with you in My Father's kingdom.*"—(Matt. xxvi. 29.)

brated in such a Church, then you may know that you are on the wrong track. *For by this shall ye know the true new Church established on earth by the Lord Himself, and not by man: that the true New Jerusalem has no need of a visible Church or edifice.* When the Lord died, the earth trembled, the rocks parted asunder, the vail of the temple was rent in twain. This signifies: *that all visible and external Church service has been rent asunder and destroyed forever.* This internal Church shines forth from every one that has received it into his heart. The ancients had but *one* Elder, and no vicarious and subordinate ecclesiastics, or any other functionaries connected with the Church; and verily I say unto you : and you may know that the true Church has no temple; wherever the Elder calls a meeting together, there is the LORD's HOUSE. Once more I say unto you, "My temple is not reared by man's hand." Thus speaks the Lord through His servant.

And now hearken unto the voice of the Lord of hosts, all ye so-called *members* of the so-called *new Churches* in America! *"All your so-called 'new Churches' shall perish through your own dissensions, through your discord, through your arrogance, your insane pride of wealth, your avarice, greediness, and spirit of vengeance, your credulity—for you lend a ready ear to calumny and slander—and that implacable hatred you show in your capacity as self-appointed judges! Any other sect or denomination is better than yours, ye proud, hypocritical Pharisees!"* Thus speaks the Lord to you through His servant.

Rome.

*And now to thee, proud Babylon, thou plague.
breathing City of seven hills, thou that art doomed
to destruction—Rome!* How great has been thy
fall, and how art thou become the habitation of
devils, and the hold of every foul spirit! For
thy sins have reached unto heaven, and God hath
remembered thy iniquities. Alas! alas! the great
city Babylon, that mighty city! for in one hour is
thy judgment come. And the kings of the earth,
who have committed fornication and lived deli-
ciously with thee, shall bewail thee and lament for
thee, when they shall see the smoke of thy burn-
ing. (Rev. xviii. 2–9.)

*And woe unto thee also, O guardian of the
towers of Babylon!* How art thou fallen; how
art thou cut down to the ground! For thou hast
said in thine heart: I will ascend into heaven, I
will exalt my throne above the stars of God. I
will sit also upon the mount of the congregation
in the sides of the north. Yet thou shalt be
brought down to hell, to the sides of the pit. Thy
pomp is brought down to the grave, and the noise
of thy viols: the worm is spread under thee, and
the worms cover thee. (Isa. xiv.) Thus saith God
the Lord, he that created the heavens and stretched
them out; he that spread forth the earth, and that
which cometh out of it; he that giveth breath
unto the people upon it, and spirit to them that
walk therein: "*I am the Lord, that is my name,*

and my glory will I not give to another, neither my praise to graven images." (Isa. xlii. 5–9.)

And yet thou hast the audacity, thou shame-faced defiler of God, *to steal the Lord's name, to steal His honor, to call thyself the vicegerent of God, and to allow thyself to be worshiped as the "Holy Father!"* Is it not written, "Neither be ye called masters; for one is your Master, even Christ, and all ye are brethren. And call no man your father upon the earth, for one is your Father which is in heaven; neither be ye called masters, for one is your master, even Christ. But he that is greatest among you shall be your servant." And is it not written, "Woe unto you, scribes and Pharisees, hypocrites; for ye compass sea and land to make one proselyte, and when he is made, ye make him twofold more the child of hell than yourselves." (Matt. xxiii. 8–15.) *Wherefore woe also unto thee, sitting on thy cursed throne; thou who art first among Pharisees and hypocrites!* The time is nigh when thou shalt go down into the infernal Jerusalem, to sit there side by side with thy predecessors, thou *" crazy Don Quixote of the Concordat,"* who art still bent on selling and destroying souls with infernal power. Take hence thy excommunicating bulls, which are the lightnings of *thy* God, even of Satan and of the Devil. Take hence the poignard and poison and every deadly weapon, the *helpmates of thy holiness,* and hurl them against thy adversaries, and thrust them against him who said: " And I have put my words in thy mouth, and I have covered thee in the shadow of mine hand, that I may plant the heavens, and lay the foundations of the earth." (Isa. li. 16.) *Better thou wouldst repent, "crux de cruce," and strew ashes on thy head, for there comes*

The End of the World,

and out of its ruins arises

The New Earth.

Dear reader, you and probably many hundreds of thousands, have been brought up from infancy in the belief that there is to be a last judgment, and that in it the earth will be for ever doomed to destruction. The Millerites, for instance, have manufactured an article of faith out of this erroneous belief. For your comfort and every one's consolation be it said:

"*That this world, this globe on which we live, shall never be destroyed, but it shall enjoy that eternal existence for which it was created.*"

This erroneous conception of "*the end of the world and of the last judgment,*" has originated from that part of the Word of the Lord where it is written: "And then shall appear the sign of the Son of Man in heaven; and then shall all the tribes of the earth mourn, and they shall see the Son of Man coming in the clouds of heaven with power and great glory." (Matt. chap: xxiv. v. 30.) (Rev. chap. xxii.) Now there exists in all the various Christian Churches a belief according to the letter of the Word, that the Lord, in His advent for the last judgment, shall actually come in person, in the clouds of heaven, with angels and the sound of trumpets; that he shall gather together all those who shall be living on the earth at that time, and the departed likewise, and that He shall cast the wicked, or the goats, down to hell, but the righteous, or the sheep, He shall gather into heaven. Then He shall make a new visible heaven, and a new earth, and on this He will cause to descend the city called the "New Jerusalem," etc.; and in this new city shall be gathered the elect, the living, as well as all the dead from the beginning of the world. The dead shall arise from their graves in their bodies, and enjoy eternal felicity in that magnificent city. You will soon learn, dear reader, if you follow attentively, how greatly in error all those persons are who believe in the above.

The second advent of the Lord is not an advent for the sake of destroying the visible heavens, and for the creation of a new habitable earth; it is not for the purpose of destroying, but for building up; therefore also salvation and not damnation is meant, "for God sent not His Son into the world to condemn the world, but that the world through him might be saved." (John chap. iii. v. 17. Matt. ch. xviii. v. 11.) The purpose of the second advent of the Lord is no other than to separate good from evil, and those having believed and still believing in Him shall be saved; and they shall be employed in building up the new angelic heaven and the New Church in the worlds. *Wherefore also the advent of the Lord, which in fact has already taken place, will not be in person, as many believe, but in the Word.* For *the Word* is the *Lord Himself.* (John chap. vii. v. 1–14.) The *spiritual* sense of the Word having been entirely lost, it became necessary for the establishment of the New Church to re-open this internal spiritual sense, and thus to provide once more a possibility for a conjunction with the Lord. This actually came to pass at the end of the first half of the eighteenth century, through an instrument selected by the Lord Himself, to whom He revealed Himself in person, and whom He filled with His spirit, that he might by means of the key or clue to the spiritual sense of the Word which was given him, proclaim the doctrines of the New Church, and make them understood. *This is the second advent of the Lord in the clouds of heaven, which has already taken place.*

By means of this clue, dear soul, will it now be possible to explain the coming of the Lord in the clouds of heaven with power and glory, etc. For according to the correspondence or typical meaning given by means of the clue above spoken of, we must understand " clouds of heaven " as meaning the Word in its spiritual sense, and " power " meaning the might of the Lord by means of the Word.

And in the same spiritual sense we must understand also by " *end of the world,*" the dying away of all old Churches ; and by " *new earth,*" the formation of the *New Church* on earth. But in order that this New Church, already established by the Lord, may not only exist on earth, but extend all over the globe, and thus spread over the whole universe ; *it is necessary that previously all should be removed and destroyed from this earth, which could be a hindrance in the way of the divine purpose.* Now, this New Church being the kingdom of the celestial good and truth, it is also the kingdom of love and justice, the kingdom of the regeneration and everlasting peace. Wherefore, also, all men who, on account of their evils and falsities, cannot become better, must be destroyed from the earth, so that the seed of evil and falsity may not again be perpetuated. And with them must disappear all that which has an infernal correspondence with the state of such men, that is to say, the causes of evil ; hence the actual condition of the whole earth and all that is thereon. And in the same measure as these states of evil and falsity in mankind are destroyed, in the same proportion shall the states of truth and goodness take root among men, and because planted in a soil made ready to receive them, they shall continue to grow. And in the same measure must everything change, both the nature and constitution of this globe and all that is thereon. And to be brief, *everything on earth must become new*, in relation to the new, that is the regenerated race of man. These necessary periodical changes of the globe and its inhabitants, come to pass by means of *revolutions, wars, famine, pestilence, earthquakes, etc.*

Therefore it is necessary that this infernal Popery and all the priesthood should be destroyed, in short all old religious institutions; besides the idle, false teachers, the priests, it will also become indispensable that their abettors, who are the emperors, kings, and other rulers, should disappear. In fact, the whole corrupt race of the higher or privileged classes, all unjust judges, all unrighteous lawyers, all dishonest merchants, all who have risen by rapacity and avarice, and everything which conflicts with love and truth. And now hearken, thou Sodom and Gomorrah among the cities of America, thou foul and wicked harlot! Hearken to what will happen to thee, oh

City of New York!

Let me shake the dust from my feet! Thou putrid pool of all vices and crimes—mother city of all knaves, of all rogues, usurers, thieves, robbers and murderers! Thou who art the infernal lurking-place of all iniquities and evil deeds! Thou hellish breeding-place of priestly vermin! My mouth shall speak thy future. Thou city full of the misery and wailing of the innocent victims of murder and violence that have been helplessly slaughtered and not revenged, crying to heaven for vengeance! It shall be done unto thee as was said by Isaiah: "I will punish the world for their evil, and the wicked for their iniquity; and I will cause the arrogancy of the proud to cease,

and will lower the haughtiness of the terrible. I
will make a man more precious than fine gold;
even a man than the golden wedge of Ophir.
Therefore I will shake the heavens, and the earth
shall remove out of her place, in the wrath of the
Lord of Hosts, and in the day of his fierce anger."
(Chap. xiii. v. 11–13.)

Hearken, therefore, ye Americans, to the voice
of the Lord, who speaks warningly to you through
the mouth of His servant; *just as it happened in
Naples* (December 16th, 1857), *and still worse
will it happen to the degenerated city of New York,
and also several seaport towns. New York, however, will be the first, for her vices and iniquities
are rapidly increasing. Therefore the Lord God
of Sabaoth will verily judge and destroy this City,
as well as the depths of the sea. Yea, the earth shall
open, shaken from her very foundations, and it
shall swallow you up, ye brood of usurers, with all
your sin-stained treasures! Yea, in sorrow must
He thus judge; therefore He hath sent the
warning through His faithful Son to every one,
so that ye should not wail and mourn, saying,
" He has not sent us any message concerning this."
Therefore the Old Father hath mercifully sent a
warning to every one through His Son.*

However, before this shall come to pass, there
will arise a great religious war, and there will be
great bloodshed, particularly in the State of New
York. And *fearful plagues will nearly depopulate
all America; nervous diseases, convulsions, pain-
ful and fatal affections of the throat and lungs,
pestilential ulcers, cholera and yellow fever will*

thin the population of America. Among the rich
in particular will these diseases rage. They will
attack them even when fleeing from their ill-gotten
riches, and smite them with destruction. The
poor, however, will then be blessed with health
and riches, neither of which had been their lot
before, because the rich had brought everything
into their own possession. " Yea, death will enter
through the windows of your houses and palaces,
to cut off the children from without and the young
men from the streets." (Jer. chap. ix. v. 21.) *And
many physicians will fall the first prey to the
plagues ;* for even among those who, as priests of
nature, should more than any others come near to
the nature of God, the greatest of them are the
most remote from it, on account of their crude
materialism and their unbelief. Their creed of phi-
lanthropy is infidelity, heartlessness, and the vilest
egotism. But also in

Europe

there will occur great revolutions and wars, which
will end in *a general religious war,* with all its
horrors, miseries, wailings and devastations.

And ye on your proud thrones, ye so-called
dynasties, ye ruling families of emperors and
kings, boasting yourselves that you rule by the
grace of God, while ye are *tolerated* by the Lord
only as the scourge of the people, that they may
be reminded of the *great evil* which they have

committed against the Lord by asking Him to give them a *king.* (1 Samuel xii. 17.) Ye proud Nebuchadnezzars, swollen with arrogance, who are trying to renew your crumbling thrones by murder, trying to cement your shattered crowns with the blood of men—in vain are all your pains, in vain slaughtering and strangling; for you strangle and slaughter but yourselves and your own children. For the divine spirit of liberty is pervading the whole globe like a Divine judgment. And I say unto you, every throne which has soiled its purple with the blood of man, be it only one drop, nourishes already in it the corrupting worm. And every crown which cements its pearls with the blood of man, be it only one drop, conceals already the dissolving *aqua regia* in its golden covering. For the blood of man is a very sharp and powerful aqua regia; it dissolves, absorbs and devours the best gold out of the richest crown. And the blood of man is stronger than the lightning of the clouds; stronger than the thunder of heaven. It foams and rushes on giant wings through a thousand heavens, up to the judgment seat of the Lord, crying for judgment. Like a thousand thunders it peals and sounds through a thousand clouds to the throne of the Lord, and cries and shouts for *vengeance!*

Ye crowned heads, do ye not hear the howling and roaring of the approaching storm in the wildly agitated air? Ye that do by cunning and by force, in your infernal love of dominion, rob the people of their rights, do ye not feel the shaking

of the earth under your trembling feet? Do ye
not hear the strokes of the terrible scourge in the
hands of the gigantic spirit of *universal republican-
ism*, while it makes already its third and last circuit
round the world? *Woe unto thee, woe unto thee,
woe unto thee, thou ancient Habsburg!* thou pes-
tilentially poisoned, tottering, foully corrupt house;
thou breeding-place of all hellish cruelties of
priests; thou guardian and protector of the Babylonian harlot; thou blinded dynasty in the land
of Herod! *too late comes thy forced repentance!*
The star-lit heavens, unappeased, still looks down
on thee with eyes that weep tears of blood—for
the slaughter of those God-fearing warriors for
liberty who perished in 1848. The fields of murder are still reeking with innocent blood, where
thy privileged hyenas have gorged themselves.
Passed away and judged already are thy bloody
tools and executioners—Windischgraetz, Haynau,
Jellacich. Thy time too is nigh, thou miserable,
cursed, tottering House. The storm is coming, and
thy columns are falling to the ground!

*Woe, O woe also to thee, thou man seated on the
usurped throne of France!* Thou who darest
destroy the work of thy great blessed ancestor,
Napoleon the First! Twice already hast thou, in
thy foolishly proud presumption, broken down the
ramparts which he had reared for the protection
of his beloved people and beloved France. But
the third time it will not avail thee, if thou dost
not tear thyself away from the Babylonian harlot
of the City of the seven hills. For if thou dost

not return to thy former benign purpose of making the people happy; if thou dost not rekindle it in thy soul withered by pride, and become a protector of the people in their holy rights by the grace of God, thou shalt suddenly fall down from thy polluted throne! Thou mayest consider it a great mercy of the Lord if, for the sake of thy ancestor, thou dost succeed in flying with thy riches to the free soil of America! For there will be no other individual like *Home* to reveal to thee, through the aid of infernal spirits, any secret republican conspiracies, secret powder magazines and other ammunitions. Thou wilt not be warned again, as it once happened, when so many innocents suffered. This *Home* is a true arch-villain of all secret vices, and a wicked plunderer of golden honors, possessing infernal magic arts, which were inoculated into him when a child by an old Egyptian, who, by so doing, unburdened himself of them. These spirits at his command were once the servants of kings. They are fallen impostors; they are as full of iniquity now as they were when they held their lying and cheating offices whilst alive. They have not yet come to their senses, nor do they repent in the spiritual world. These hardened and obdurate spirits can be exercised only for magical purposes; but the good spirits weep over those poor souls who have allowed themselves to fall under the influence of these wicked spirits, and pray day and night to the Lord to save these poor beings (grandees). Thou too, Emperor of France, wilt be sacrificed ignominiously through those lying spirits, if thou dost not repent. *Never shouldst thou have usurped the crown*, and thou wouldst have been a true follower of thy great ancestor, who would have loved and revered thee. Why didst thou not go to those who have warned thee once already, and shown thee the "*new morning star ?*"

Why hast thou not consulted those through whom the world has been saved from the evil, and through whom each one finds his salvation ? From those spirits who but meditate fälsity and evil, there shines no "*light of peace through the clear morning air.*" SAPIENTI SAT!

And thou, reigning House of Prussia, much would I have to say also to thee, but thou dost not deserve it. Thou hast sold the best blood of thy house, and betrayed and cast helplessly into the world one beloved of the Lord. What has become of Henrietta Caroline, the daughter of Prince Henry of Prussia, who died in Rome? Great and heavy evil have ye committed against this orphan, sacrificed heartlessly to your arrogant pride; but the Father of all orphans has royally rewarded her; He will soon summon you to give account before His judgment seat. Your insane haughtiness and pride is your destruction.

Once more take heed, all ye crowned heads; put your houses in order; for the Lord of Hosts, the Lord of Sabaoth, is Himself the warrior for:

The Great Republic of the World.

Be silent now, ye bells of alarm! Ye holy, golden-stringed harps of peace, murmur softly in sweet strains of blissful harmony and rest! With your heart-comforting and soul-elevating notes impart strength to the weak, comfort the desponding, animate the warriors for the victory which is nigh! Praise the Lord! *For after having destroyed the City of New York by earthquakes, and raised from the mysterious deep, by the same commotions, "*THE NEW CALIFORNIA,*" a land of gold, for the natural use of His faithful,—He will build up through His grace, on the golden land, a new city for His faithful of America. This new city will be called "*THE NATURAL NEW JERUSALEM.*" And thousands of ye true-hearted, noble Americans will flock to it, to behold the* NEW CHURCH, *the* HOLY CITY, *and the temple therein, and there to pray in spirit and in truth, which means to act. And peace and harmony will reign in the New City of the Lord. The worst murderers and evil doers will be converted and become good men, the moment they are allowed to tread this soil. And there will be such an abundance of natural riches, that from its plenty there will be allotted enough to each one; then there will be no poverty and no sickness, and never more will there be seen a dimmed and tearful eye !!!*

Thus speaks the Lord to all the best of you Americans, through His faithful son and servant, who exultingly exclaïms: *Praise the Lord with the sound of trumpets, for truly He loves you all! Give glory! glory! glory! in the dawn of the morning to*

The New great Republic of the World!!

And glory! glory! glory! to

The Holy New Jerusalem!!!

———————

WRITTEN OCTOBER, 1868.

www.ingramcontent.com/pod-product-compliance
Lightning Source LLC
Chambersburg PA
CBHW021128020726
47500CB00003B/969